Caring
for
Stan

A Story for Anyone
Who Knows Someone
with Alzheimer's

alzheimer's association

Northern California & Northern Nevada
182 El Dorado Street
Monterey, CA 93940
(831) 647-9890; (831) 757-0531

Caring for Stan
A Story for Anyone Who Knows Someone with Alzheimer's

Written by Joanne Damours

Library of Congress Control Number: 2010902816
ISBN: 978-0-578-05174-1
Printed in the United States of America

Dedicated to Stan

Table of Contents

Acknowledgements

I would like to thank the caregivers who generously shared their stories with me, especially Hilda Coleman and Deanne Michaloski. I thank my father, who taught me to recognize a good story, and my mother, who encouraged me to look below the surface of life. Thank you to Charlene Thurston, Director of Palliative and Supportive Care of Nantucket, MA, whose wisdom, humor, and honesty inspired me. Thank you to Suzanne Daub, my editor and coach. Thank you to my friend Susan Silverman who patiently listened as I used her as a sounding board. Thank you to Marta Allen and other members of my writers' group who listened to my manuscript and provided invaluable comments. Thank you to my children, step-children, children-in-law, and grandchildren for their many contributions. And special thanks to two of my friends, a brother and a sister, whose care for their mother showed me what love could be.

Introduction

Writing has always been difficult for me and, other than rearing my children, caregiving was an activity I never considered. To find myself caregiver for my husband Stan, who has Alzheimer's Disease, and writing a book about my experiences, was completely unexpected.

In my early years of caregiving, I read every book on Alzheimer's that I could find. Many books were helpful in broadening my understanding, but I didn't find a book that was a candid first-hand description of the issues caregivers face. This is such a book, and I hope others will find it helpful.

If you have recently lost a friend or family member or have Alzheimer's yourself, you may find reading this book difficult. My humor is not meant to offend. What seems amusing to a seasoned caregiver in the midst of caregiving may not seem amusing to you.

Throughout the book I've referred to the person with Alzheimer's as "he" and the caregiver as "she."

This was not meant to diminish women who are caring for women and men who are caregivers. This is my story, and it was easiest to tell it in this way.

"Loved one" is often used to describe a person with a disease. I've avoided that phrase and used "patient" instead. Although I have always loved Stan, there have been many times I felt the opposite. "Loved one" didn't seem completely honest.

I hope caregivers will be more comfortable being themselves after reading this book and that others will come away with a deeper understanding of what caregivers experience. I've learned that caregiving is not an activity you succeed at. You muddle through, dealing with ambiguity and uncertainty. Guilt and discouragement are part of the journey, and those around a caregiver can help immensely by offering encouragement and respect.

I am relatively young to be a caregiver for someone with Alzheimer's and probably more energetic than most. No one should feel guilty if he or she is unable to care for someone as long into the disease as I have. Everyone is different and every circumstance is different.

I've made a few small adjustments to chronology and left out some events to move the story along, but this is how it happened. I expect you'll be surprised at times and maybe even smile.

Joanne Damours

Chapter 1

Out of Denial

Stan came into my office and asked, "You're my wife, aren't you?" "Yes," I replied. He asked, "Will you tell me what's been going on for the last 20 years?"

The realization that something is wrong can come in many ways, sometimes slowly and sometimes suddenly. A person may ask the same question over and over, forgetting each time that he asked it before. Or like my friend, whose husband sent his pickup truck hurtling down a 200 foot hill, impacting a tree and barely missing fishermen in the lake below, the realization can be sharp and jolting.

For me it was sudden. Later I realized there had been clues. I'd made excuses: we're getting older... we're stressed, but when the moment came I was shocked.

"How do I get to downtown San Pedro from here?" Stan asked. He was driving my car around the suburbs of Washington DC, following roads familiar to both of us. For many years Stan had spent ten days out of each month driving these same roads. The rest of the month he was in California. But now, here in our space, Washington, he was asking an unthinkable question.

It took a few seconds to sink in and my stomach clenched. Holding myself tightly in control, I said, "What you just asked worries me."

Over the next few days I pulled myself out of denial. I allowed myself to watch and see what was happening with Stan.

Stan was 59 and I was 48 when we met at a risk assessment seminar in Colorado. By the time we were married, more than nine years had passed. Nine years filled with many joys, sorrows, and problems. There never was much doubt that we belonged together. At the time Stan asked that question, we had been married for two years, but still living on two coasts. Stan's five grown children lived in California. My four grown children, mother, and business were on the East Coast. Married, we spent about a third of our time together but still lived three thousand miles apart.

No one I knew had ever had serious memory problems and I'd never considered the possibility. My mother was notably absent-minded as I was growing up. It wasn't unusual to find strange objects, pots and pans, in the refrigerator. Now, she was in remission from cancer, 85, sharp and making all the decisions about her own care.

My father had spent about two years in a nursing home before he died. He too had been sharp to the end and, when visiting him, I'd contrasted his alertness with the strange robotlike behavior of the Alzheimer's patients.

It never occurred to me what marrying someone 69-years-old could mean. I had always imagined Stan dying of a heart attack while making love, his favorite activity.

I felt unprepared and betrayed. It had taken a long time to find Stan and now something very frightening was happening. I was angry that he was messing it up. Stan should be healthy—He never drank, never smoked, rarely ate sugar, and worked out vigorously every day.

Later when I talked to his colleagues, they said they began noticing problems four years earlier. Politeness, fear, or some unspoken rule of our society prevents people from speaking out. Afraid they might say something "wrong," they let their concern pass and live with an uncomfortable feeling that maybe they should have said something.

They are probably right about people's reactions. A few months after I realized there was a problem, two of Stan's colleagues asked me out to dinner without Stan. One of them was a medical doctor. "You must do something and do it now. Don't wait. You must get him to the best specialists." They were much more polite, but by the time the dinner was over, I felt beaten up. Out of some misguided desire to please, I had paid for the dinner. I wondered why I'd paid to feel so miserable.

But Stan's friends had spoken the truth and I was grateful they had. Stan did need to see a doctor or many doctors. We had to do something and right away. Later Stan would have flashes of clarity. He would send me reeling with a comment like, "Help me! Something's wrong with my mind!" But at that time, he didn't seem aware that he had a problem. He distrusted doctors. He refused to see one.

Chapter 2

Reactions

"It'll never happen to me. I'll jump off a cliff first,"
Stan said after I described the effects of Alzheimer's.
"What if you forget to jump?" I asked.

I remember standing on the beach about that time, feeling the waves washing over my feet, eroding my solid footing, threatening my balance, replacing what was there with what was not. How like my feelings, I noted.

Trying to think clearly, I asked Stan to make a doctor's appointment in California. He refused. I begged. He didn't listen.

I called his youngest daughter who lived near him in southern California and asked for her help. I asked an older daughter who lived in northern California to talk to him, to convince him to see a doctor. Neither strategy worked. The huge inefficiencies of living so far apart began to sink in. Most of the time Stan had come to the East Coast to see me. Now I had to go to the West Coast to help him.

A series of doctors' visits and tests began. Usually I made the appointment, then flew to California to drag Stan to the doctor's office. First we visited the primary care physician, then neurologists. He had an EKG, EEG, MRI, and CAT scan. At Stan's level of the disease, nothing was conclusive—diagnoses contradicted each other and everyone seemed to have some advice.

More questions filled my mind than I was able to process. What's wrong? Should he drive? Is there a cure? Will he be like the Alzheimer's patients I had seen at my father's nursing home? Can I handle this?

Waves of numbness would come over me followed by periods of frantic activity searching the internet and making telephone calls. Finally a neurologist suggested Stan get neuropsychological testing. "Neuropsych" testing takes four to six hours and is composed of many small tests of different cognitive aspects of the mind. The testing is performed by a trained psychologist, is expensive, and isn't covered by Medicare or most medical plans.

After the neuropsych testing, only a medical doctor can legally make a diagnosis. The psychologist cannot. The psychologist who tested Stan called me. "I can't officially say, but it's almost certainly Alzheimer's," he said. Two of the tests, short term memory and spacial orientation, are clear indicators. Stan did abysmally on both of them.

It took another three years for a medical doctor, a neurologist, to finally say, "It's Alzheimer's." I suppose their reluctance to make a diagnosis is understandable. Alzheimer's can only be definitively diagnosed after death in an autopsy, and it's just one of over 100 forms of dementia.

During this period a huge void opened in our marriage. Up until then we had talked about everything, shared our secrets, and felt deeply connected. Now Stan seemed oblivious to a problem that was consuming my life. Half the people I talked to suggested that I discuss it with him and the other half warned against it. I tried talking to him. He denied having any problems. I saw the implications of his diagnosis and knew what it would mean in the long term. I wanted him to understand how it was affecting me. Eventually I decided it was best not to talk to him about Alzheimer's, but my anger didn't listen. I'd push it down and try to placate myself with thoughts like, "What a wonderful blessing it is to care for someone you love! " And later I'd yell at him, "How can you do this to me?"

I remember going to an Alzheimer's caregiver support group some time later. The leader asked how many of the caregivers in the room were angry about their situation. Everyone in the room raised her hand. I was in a "wonderful blessing" frame of mind and was about to be the only one not to raise her hand. "Oh, yes," I said to myself as I connected with my anger, "I'm furious."

Stunned is probably the best way to describe Stan's children's initial reaction. Later came a sense of heartwrenching loss. Their mother had died many years earlier and they adored their father.

As the family discussions moved from initial reactions to Stan's long term care, two of Stan's five children reassured me that there were facilities where Stan could be placed. They told me they supported my doing that when it was needed. Stan's oldest son was in business for himself and offered his help organizing Stan's finances. His youngest daughter began researching natural cures. Another daughter was living outside the country and offered her prayers.

My children were also stunned but for different reasons. Though they liked Stan, they'd never had a chance to bond with him as a father. Their concern was for me. The statistics are bad for caregivers of Alzheimer's patients, especially women under 65 caring for an older spouse. Caregivers in that category are about 20% more likely to die than non-caregivers. My children were worried about me. They were afraid for me. They were concerned that I wouldn't be there to play a part in their and their children's lives.

As I listened, I began to develop a deeper understanding. Each family has its own culture with unseen rules and assumptions. Stan's family, like many others, valued entrepreneurship and autonomy. His children felt Stan would want them to move on with their lives and, while providing support, have someone else manage day-to-day issues and care. In my family, though we paid little or no attention to passing illnesses, if someone was in critical need, we mobilized. We gave it our all, no matter how resentful we might be, how stressed, or how much we had to sacrifice.

Stan and I had been married for two years. I knew he loved me, but I suspected that at some level he'd realized before we were married that he had a problem. I suspected he had seen me as something of a safety net. Later I met two other women who had the same experience. Almost exactly two years after marrying an older man, each one came face-to-face with Alzheimer's.

I felt unfairly used and afraid that I couldn't handle the challenges of caregiving. Yet my love for Stan, my convictions, and family programming required me to commit to care for him. At that time I began a long journey out of myself, across the void that had developed in our relationship and toward a place where compassion and understanding predominated. We all need and want to be cared for. We are all afraid.

Chapter 3

Patient's Rights

A mathematician, Stan told people at the adult day care center, "I think I have zero to two wives."

We went out to eat at an Italian restaurant. The next morning very early, Stan woke me and asked, "Are we behind enemy lines?" I said, "No." He asked, "Aren't we in Italy?" I repeated, "No," then realized what he was thinking. I told him, "The war is over and we won!" He sighed with relief.

Stan was born in Brooklyn, a rough and conflicted atmosphere in the 1930s. Each neighborhood, every block, had its own set of immigrants. There were the Irish, Italian, and Jewish blocks, close to each other and struggling to coexist and adjust to American life. Most of the stress was expressed through the children who formed informal ethnic groups and battled with each other. Stan always said he was too Jewish to get along with the children from other groups and not Jewish enough to get along with his. His crush on an Irish girl and her rejection played out in our relationship. He always thought of me as Irish, though as a totally blended WASP, my minimal Irish blood had long been diluted. No amount of telling him the truth could change his mind.

His two older brothers played a key role in his life. The brothers were about a year apart in age and ten years older than Stan. Stan's mother was disappointed that he wasn't the girl she'd hoped for. A sense that he wasn't quite what other people wanted settled over him from an early age.

And those older brothers, they were gods. Stan strove for their attention and affection. As a young boy he admiringly watched one of his brothers cook bacon on the hot coal furnace in the basement. His mother had relented that far, allowing bacon in the basement. By the time Stan was a teenager, the kosher kitchen was forgotten. After a quick bar mitzvah with only his parents and a rabbi present, Stan never again practiced the religion.

It's strange how people perceive their childhoods. Stan's older brother tells of a happy childhood. Stan always turned dark when talking about his, communicating a time of stress and anxiety.

Perhaps the darkness Stan felt was the war, World War II, which began when he was eleven. Fear for relatives known and unknown filled the Jewish community as rumors of horrors flowed. His older brothers enlisted in the Navy and were sent to the European front. Stan's memories of this time focused on his mother crying uncontrollably at the kitchen table, filled with fear that her two boys would never return home.

The family's favorite place was the beach. Stan's mother loved the sand, waves, and water. She took Stan to Coney Island every weekend in the summer, and he learned to love the ocean too.

By the time Stan started school, his parents, immigrants from the Ukraine, realized that education was the key to success in America. Their two oldest boys had slipped by without them understanding this important fact, and they were determined not to let that happen with Stan. Never in doubt that he would attend college, Stan still found himself unprepared as he stood in line to register at City College. On the registration form was a space to declare a major course of study. At that moment, Stan made a decision that would profoundly affect his life. He wanted to sign up for a curriculum in psychology, but he didn't know how to spell "psychology." He signed up for engineering instead.

Stan's career in engineering and later in applied mathematics was stellar. He received his doctorate, developed the first mathematical approach to risk assessment, and was awarded many honors. His main strategy for success was to "go back to basics." He approached every problem with fresh and unprejudiced eyes and did so by consciously cultivating what he called "forgetting." "Forgetting" caused problems in his personal life, but the professional advantages more than compensated. Much later when he could no longer solve mathematical problems by starting with basics, his colleagues immediately realized he was failing.

In 1960 Stan moved his family from the East Coast to California. He was smitten. He fell in love with the sun, beaches, and sense of boundless possibilities that was so much a part of the California mystique at that time. Attracted to a healthy lifestyle from the time he was a child, Stan scuba dived and jogged along beaches. He had found his paradise.

Stan loved music. He loved to sing and had a beautiful resonating baritone voice. This was the man, kind and gentle, strong in his convictions, I fell in love with.

A current trend is to think about and write documents on "rights": children's rights, human rights, and patient's rights. I've read a patient's rights document that I found attached to the end of a tall stack of papers given to me when Stan was admitted to a hospital. Patients have a right to know what's going on and what their diagnosis is. They have the right to be treated with respect. Doctors follow protocols to ensure the rights are observed. They ask, "Do you understand what I just told you?"

I was angry. As far as I was concerned, Stan had absolutely no rights. Put another way, if he was going to get a disease like Alzheimer's, and if I was going to take care of him for ten to fifteen years experiencing all the horrors described in books, then he had just forfeited every right he ever had. And put still another way, I wanted him to move to the East Coast where my family and friends lived. My mother was on the East Coast fighting cancer. Besides, it wouldn't be long before he couldn't understand what a doctor said.

As my anger faded, I realized that on some level I'd understood that the wellbeing of the caregiver is the key to successful management of Alzheimer's. Stan's wellbeing depended on mine. He did have rights, but mine, the caregiver's, were just as important. When one person becomes dependent on another, that other person becomes responsible for the wellbeing of two.

In my mind, Stan's love for California and desire to be near his children had become a low priority. Besides, someone was going to get hurt and it was only a question of whom. If we lived on the West Coast, my children and grandchildren would see less of me and I of them. My business would probably suffer. If we lived on the East Coast, Stan's children would be far away. He would be stuck in a part of the country that had come to symbolize his unhappy childhood and the limits and restrictions of life.

His children came together to visit us and expressed how much they wanted to have their father nearby. Wanting to please them, knowing how much Stan loved them and California, I considered the battle I would have keeping Stan on the East Coast. He was still able to drive. With help making an airline reservation and getting to the airport, he could still fly. If someone picked him up at a destination and dropped him off at the airport, he could still attend a professional meeting in another part of the country and provide some useful insight.

I considered moving west. Denial set in again and I forgot the stories I'd read of the demands on the caregivers of Alzheimer's patients. I visualized myself hopping on planes and traveling to see my children and my mother. My self-image as a resourceful, can-do person, solving problems, making new friends, filled my mind. I lost touch with reality and decided to move to California.

Chapter 4

Love Reaches Out

As my mother was dying, she said, "Love reaches out everywhere."

After selling or giving away most of my furniture and belongings, I packed what remained and shipped it to California. Turning back was no longer an option. I had put Stan and his family first and planned to use my resourcefulness to make the move work for me, my family, and my business.

Stan and I were in Baltimore standing in line to board the airplane that was the final step in the move. I was feeling confident that I'd made the right decision when my cell phone rang. It was my mother. In a shaky voice she told me that she was out of remission, that the cancer was back. This was the fourth time it had returned. Each time her remissions had been shorter. She was 86 and the odds did not seem good.

Living on adrenalin for the next year, I went through all the physical and mental resources I had.

After a short stay in California, I took Stan with me to stay with my mother. Leaving him behind wasn't an option anymore. Left alone, he forgot pots on the stove and ate moldy food from the refrigerator. Telling him how much I needed his emotional support, I hoped he'd stay without a fight. Arriving to visit my mother, she commented that I had two suitcases instead of the usual one. "I've come to stay for as long as you need me," I told her.

Resources for my mother seemed readily available. I was one of them. I gave up my life, or took it with me, and arrived on the scene. Hospice provided wonderful support. Nurses came to my mother's house to show me what to do, and answers to questions seemed relatively clear. My mother was able to make all the decisions. Though I disagreed sometimes, I was along for the ride and it was her show. I did everything I could for her including getting a puppy, her last wish. She said she'd always wanted a puppy and my father had only let her have cats.

Ten months after the cancer returned and as she was dying in the hospital, she shared profound images. She said, "Life is beautiful and all those people, you think they're gone, but they're still there." For the first time I was able to see my mother as a person, separate from her role in my life. I liked her and admired her.

After my mother died, I found myself exhausted and my immune system deeply compromised. Colds, flu, exhaustion dominated my life for many months as I returned to California and turned my attention to Stan. As I regained my health, I realized I was in big trouble.

The strategies that had worked well in caring for my mother were not going to work with Stan. If I tried to care for him with the same intensity I'd used with my mother, I'd burn out and die long before he did. Alzheimer's has a nickname of the "ten year disease" because the patient often lives ten, though sometimes fifteen or more, years after diagnosis. It's a disease that provides plenty of time for a caregiver to self-destruct, plenty of time for self-doubt and depression. Running on adrenalin is not an option.

My resolution to care for Stan dissolved in my exhaustion and grief. Stan's children came to visit and I held their hands, sobbing, "I don't think I can do it." Then "I'll try, but, when I can't go on, I'll give him back to you."

Chapter 5

Mood Disturbances

After attending an adult day care center for a few months and enjoying the karaoke, Stan decided he didn't want to go anymore. When I asked him why, he said it wasn't progressing his singing career.

"**I** pace myself," my 80 year old aunt said when I asked her how she coped with my uncle's Alzheimer's. Overloading and enjoying the rush of upcoming deadlines had been my lifestyle. To even begin to take care of Stan, I'd have to learn to pace myself. Pacing would be a new experience.

I devised a concept I called "baseline living." Baseline living was when you're so current with tasks that you wake up on a Saturday morning and wonder what you'll do all day. I cut back on commitments, streamlined my life, and busied myself with "catching up." Many months later I realized I was still catching up. That empty Saturday never came.

I began obsessing about organization. Purchasing books on decluttering, I pondered colored file folders and storage cubes. Feeling more in control of my outer environment, I realized that inside I was just as stressed as before.

On the other hand, Stan seemed happy. We walked along the beach looking at the sunrise every morning. I think he felt a certain satisfaction that he'd finally succeeded in getting me to move to California and a perverse part of me wondered if he had gotten Alzheimer's as a subconscious strategy.

Outwardly denying anything was wrong, Stan showed his anxiety by panicking when he couldn't see me. When I was in the bathroom, he'd tear out the front door not knowing where I was and determined to find me. When I'd come out of the bathroom and look for him, I'd find him outdoors, sometimes walking down the street.

The stress was increasing. I was grieving my mother and my dreams of Stan's and my life together. I'd visualized moving to California many times and none of those dreams had looked like this. My efforts to pace myself were not working. I was sinking, depressed and adrift.

"A support group is what you need," people advised. Finally listening, I tried some. "My spouse died a year ago." "Mine died three years ago." Surprised, I realized that most of the people at one group were grieving. Later I heard the group disbanded when the last patient died. "Only feelings," the leader of another group insisted. Exchanging information about the disease and practical advice was forbidden. I wanted information too and knew that group wouldn't work for me. "Don't let him drive!" several people shouted at me at another group. Stan's doctor said it was up to me to decide if it was safe for him to drive. I still thought it was.

I may have been more needy than other caregivers. The group I settled on consisted of the leader and me, two people.

I'd probably been in denial about Stan's driving. Early one morning on the way to the beach, confusing the accelerator for the brakes, Stan raced to full speed through a red light. I sat in the passenger seat horrified. There had been no other cars, no pedestrians early that morning. We and the car survived. No one else was hurt. A caregiver can educate herself on the strange and frightening behaviors to expect with Alzheimer's. Then years pass. Good caregiving is providing as much autonomy as possible for as long as possible. The caregiver often recognizes a problem after something bad happens and then remembers she should have expected it.

Stan was relentless. Hiding the car keys upset him. He'd ask for my help finding them and I'd spend hours pretending to search for them. I developed a strategy. When he wanted to go somewhere, I'd drop whatever I was doing. "Please, please, please let me drive!" I'd beg. "I love this car!" I'd gush. Stan proudly offered driving tips as I drove and he sat next to me. Only after several years did he realize he wasn't driving anymore and wonder why.

I could still leave him alone at home. We had only one car. He couldn't drive if I took it when I left.

Coming home one night after an evening with new friends, I found Stan's shoes in the garage, soaking wet. "What happened?" I asked. "I walked into the swimming pool," he said. "I didn't see it in the dark." The implications sank in as I realized he could no longer be left alone. His safety—his life—depended on it, and I was responsible.

Now having to watch Stan almost continuously, I discovered adult day care centers. "Respite" is a word that is used to mean a short vacation from the 24-hour responsibility of caring for someone ill. I needed respite.

Karaoke, standing before an audience, holding a microphone, singing in his beautiful baritone, pleased Stan at first. As the novelty wore off, he began to complain about the "old" and "decrepit" people, not realizing he was older and looked worse than many of them. The facilities were excellent. The staff was wonderful, but his extreme attachment to me meant I had to trick him into going. "Please, for me," I begged. It worked twice. I'd sneak into the day care center and hide while a staff member went out to the car. They'd enthusiastically greet Stan, and escort him out of the car into the center. That worked four or five times. Driving different routes to the center worked for a month or two. "Where are we going?" he'd ask angrily when he suspected where we were headed.

Standing with a determined face and straining to escape, I could see Stan at the door when I picked him up. In the background I'd see the staff person who was holding onto him. Eventually, a full time volunteer was needed to keep him inside the center. I was the most vulnerable link in the chain of his care. Guilt over-whelmed me from time to time, but I pushed it away and continued to trick him. Respite was essential.

"Love. Patience. Muscles. Sense of Humor. En-durance. If They're Wearing Thin, Call Us!" I stood in the kitchen and contemplated this slogan. It was on a refrigerator magnet given to me by the local Caregiver Resource Center. Funded by the state of California, the center acts as a clearing house, identifying caregivers in trouble and providing information to them. Caring for caregivers is good. It also saves money. Without caregivers, the responsibility and cost often falls on the state.

I'd contacted the Center soon after I moved to California and they'd tested me for depression. "Mood disturbances" they'd said. Tested six months later, "mood disturbances" again, not depressed, but not nor-mal either. They'd said I was doing everything right, going to a support group, adult day care, simplifying my life. Why did I feel so terrible? Since no one was rushing to help me, to show me what to do with Stan, I reasoned there were a lot of people out there worse off than me.

Chapter 6

Relationship Troubles

Stan asked, "Who are you?" We were married, but I was feeling playful and decided to test his reactions. "I'm your new girlfriend." "Where did I meet you?" he asked. "In a bar at one-o-clock in the morning," I joked. He looked puzzled but didn't say anything. I waited a few seconds then said, "That's not true, we met at the synagogue." "Oh!" he said. "I know that's not true because I never go to the synagogue!"

After driving from Michigan to the East Coast, 800 miles, on a Friday night, my brother installed a new faucet in my mother's bathroom. He exchanged a few words with her and drove back to Michigan in time for work Monday. I was providing hands-on care for my mother during her struggle with cancer but never doubted that my brother supported me and was helping in every way possible. Later he handled the details of her estate, something I couldn't. Not everyone gives in the same way.

Now I had huge doubts about the support of the people around me. Like many other caregivers of

Alzheimer's patients, my relationships were crumbling. I felt isolated and alone. When my mother had cancer, problems seemed immediate and the family mobilized. This disease was trudging on and on, year after year.

My children lived far away on the East Coast. They were angry with Stan's children for not doing more to help. They were busy with their own lives.

After my mother died and I inherited the family home, I'd felt that a few of my children's comments about use of the property were inappropriate and insensitive. It seemed to me that they were trying to make decisions that were mine to make. I overreacted. "I'm not dead yet," I said. Now I wondered if I'd gone too far, if I'd alienated them.

Stan's youngest daughter lived close by. She felt that she understood her father's wishes better than I did and disapproved of the care I was giving. "You're a liar," she said to me. To convince Stan to take his medications, I called them vitamins.

She had promised her father she would take care of him and, having read a book that promised a cure for Alzheimer's, she wanted to take him away to the mountains for three weeks. She planned to take him off his medications, stimulate his mind with mental exercises and singing, and feed him a special diet. She hoped she could heal him. I imagined her bringing him back and saying, "Sorry it didn't work." Taking Alzheimer's patients off their medications doesn't shorten their lives, but often results in a dramatic and permanent decline—Stan and I could spend many years paying the price if her experiment failed.

I didn't have the whole picture, it turned out. In my exhaustion after my mother's death, I'd told Stan's children that I'd "try" to care for him and, if I couldn't, I'd give Stan to them. As my energy came back, my commitment to care for him had grown, but I'd neglected to tell them I'd changed my mind. I no longer felt "required" to care for Stan. I wanted to care for him. I hadn't understood that his daughter planned to take responsibility for his care, if I agreed to the plan and if Stan got worse.

"She's his daughter," I reminded myself in my down moments. I wondered why I was continuing a relationship with someone who seemed to dislike me and who disapproved of what I was doing. But she had a point. Early in Stan's disease I'd searched for cures, studying diets, vitamin supplements, medical research. Hope is required to be a healer. Acceptance is required to be a caregiver. Trying to balance both proved too much for me and I finally settled into my role as caregiver. You could say I gave up. If I thought too much about cures, I cried. If I felt a little hope, I was afraid I'd be disappointed. She'd persevered. There may be a link between Alzheimer's and diet. Mental stimulation may prevent it.

Besides, there's a genetic predisposition to Alzheimer's. If one of my parents had had the disease, I'd probably want to try anything that promised a cure.

Facing Alzheimer's is difficult. When Stan's rambling out-of-context comments took over telephone conversations, his sons stopped calling. Men tend to like problems that can be solved. When his sons asked for a progress report, there was no progress.

To be fair, Stan's children visited us. He may not have recognized them individually, but he found their presence reassuring and familiar. In spite of our differences, Stan's youngest daughter graciously cared for him one evening a week so I could spend some time with friends. His oldest daughter continued to call regularly and kindly listened to me vent. Her father-in-law had died of Alzheimer's and she understood the disease and caregiver problems better than the others. Another of Stan's daughters, struggling with caring for an autistic child, kept us in her prayers.

"Do you want to have a relationship with your grandchildren?" At a vulnerable moment, I received an e-mail from my son and his wife and interpreted it as an ultimatum. My grandson and I had had a favorite table in a local restaurant where we'd enjoyed one-on-one dinners. We'd taken karate lessons together. Now my granddaughter hardly knew who I was. My imagined trips to the East Coast had not materialized.

I replied angrily. A few e-mail exchanges and the damage was done. Several months of silence between us passed, more isolation and plenty of time for me to think. I'd interpreted the e-mail in the context of my own exhaustion. They had just wanted me to be in my grandson's and granddaughter's lives.

My son had suggested I see a psychologist and it seemed a good idea. "I'm a caregiver for my husband who has Alzheimer's and my son isn't speaking to me," was all that was needed to be offered an appointment the next day. As I read the e-mails to the psychologist, she pointed out that words like "always" and "never" pop up when we're in a child state. Adult life is subtle, uncertain, given to complex motives, needs and desires. The psychologist conducted another test for depression. Mood disturbances again. She said I was doing great, considering.

As my mother was dying, she didn't want to see or talk to anyone. Though I was managing her care, I doubt she wanted me there either. She said, "I like the visitors who don't sit down."

In our culture we have an image of a deathbed, friends and family gathered round, praying, looking sad and holding hands. My mother wanted to be alone. Tired of blocking people at the door and making excuses to keep others away, I asked the hospice nurse what I should do. "We all have a responsibility to our family and friends until the end," she said.

Negotiating with my mother, trying to respect her desire to be alone, I held my cell phone to her ear as she said, "I love you" to her grandchildren. I allowed her closest friends to make short visits. They deserved some closure too.

Now feeling isolated in California, I thought about my mother's death. I thought about my responsibilities. So many of my relationships had suffered. I was making progress learning to pace myself, but despite respite, reducing commitments and a neat house, I felt exhausted and on edge most of the time. Even so I was still alive. I'd been expecting people to rush to help me, but I had a responsibility to reach out to them too.

Chapter 7

Anxiety and Addiction

I had just returned from a short business trip to Washington DC. I drove to the adult day care center to pick up Stan who had been asking where I was. Stan didn't see me, but a staff member did. I was standing behind Stan when the staff member asked, "How much do you love your wife?" Stan answered, "16 ounces."

Having decided to take more responsibility for my relationships, I took a look at myself. In my current state, I couldn't. Stress and feelings of inadequacy seemed to fill my life. Like a tidal wave taking over my body, the anxiety would consume and overwhelm me. The wave would come on suddenly and reach a peak in a few seconds. The effect could last for hours or days, and during that time I'd be depressed. Sometimes I thought of suicide. Tests for depression usually ask about feelings in the last ten days or two weeks. The tests given to me never coincided with one of the periods when I was thinking my darkest thoughts.

During the aftermath of a wave, I'd slowly pull myself out of the depression by remembering I wasn't the only person caring for someone with Alzheimer's. I wasn't the only one who was struggling. My support group helped. Respite kept me alive.

"Firsts " were the most likely to cause a wave. The first time Stan urinated in a wastebasket. The first time he couldn't remember my name. The first time he spoke gibberish. My mother's disease had been predictable. Burned once, twice, many times, with Stan I felt I was living in a war zone, where a bomb could go off unexpectedly at any moment.

The borderline between anxiety and addiction seemed fragile. My first reaction was to stop the wave as fast as I could and that meant to drug myself. Food worked as a drug until I realized I'd gained 15 lbs. I hit the bottle a few times but felt horrible the next day.

In the past, I'd enjoyed a life of stress and thrived on the edginess of it, rushing to accomplish the unthinkable and proving to myself how competent I was. To keep the stress under control, I'd meditated, had hobbies, and kept busy. Now I felt flattened, unable to do anything without an interruption from Stan. I was constantly concerned for his safety and unable to leave him alone. Meditation seemed impossible. I was on the edge of losing control. And I did sometimes. The owner of our pool service company listened sympathetically on the phone while I sobbed over a small misunderstanding about the bill. I was crabby with salespeople. I yelled at phone solicitors.

To protect themselves from sleepless nights, health care professionals are taught to keep a distance between themselves and people with problems. I wanted to hear what a great job I was doing, every day, many times a day, by someone who really cared about me, who wasn't trying to keep a distance. Telling myself I was doing a great job wasn't enough. I was too full of a sense of inadequacy to believe my own words.

I thought about turning to my children. When I was young, I remember my mother dutifully writing two letters every week, one to her mother and one to my father's mother. Something changed in my generation. My children expected me to call them and most of the time that was more than I could handle.

I wanted the stress, the anxiety, to go away. Anything seemed better than what I was feeling. The landscape of my life would have to change dramatically before I could even think of reaching out and repairing relationships.

In one of the support groups I'd attended, the leader had distributed a list of activities for caregivers, "Tools for Releasing Stress." It listed about 100 activities, including playing softball, holding a baby, and going to a football game. I circled the ones that seemed feasible. Playing softball and going to a football game were not circled. Instead of a baby I cuddled my mother's little dog in my arms for days at a time. I wondered at my mother's wisdom in wanting a puppy just before she died. Maybe it was for me, not her.

Feeling a little better, I developed an approach. My efforts at "baseline living," completing projects, waiting for that open Saturday, had failed. I still had pending projects, some of them important, like taxes, and they were contributing to my anxiety. I decided to put Stan in day care an extra day each week while I worked on them.

Taking up an old hobby, I started knitting again. Knitting a few rows when I felt stressed calmed me. Hats were big enough, no sweaters.

Not sure whether it was an addiction or a solution, I relied on television and became good friends with the characters in my favorite shows. They were reliable, predictable, just interesting enough, and didn't require the effort of a relationship.

Then came the books. When a wave of anxiety would overtake me, I'd race to the computer and order books on Alzheimer's. Reading them reinforced the ways I was fortunate. For the most part Stan had kept his sweet nature. When he became agitated, I told him how handsome he was and how much I loved him and he calmed down immediately.

Almost angrily I determined I wasn't going to die for Stan. "Put on your oxygen mask before you put on the mask of the child next to you," caregivers are reminded at support groups. Take care of yourself. Turning my anger and frustration inward, in a subtle way, I'd been trying to hurt myself. I'd go days then realize I'd lived on caffeine, forgetting to drink even one glass of water. Knowing I had to make a change, I started paying attention to my health, exercising and eating better.

I'd always felt a little insulted when people said to me, "keep breathing," as though I would somehow stop or didn't know the basics of life. With some practice, though, I came to appreciate the wisdom in those words. If I started breathing slowly and deeply as soon as I felt a wave of anxiety start, I could often ride it out without feeling overwhelmed.

Later, after I'd made some progress, I stood at the window of an office building, looking out over a parking lot and trees. I noticed a strange feeling. I felt normal. I'd wondered if I'd ever feel normal again. Years had passed since I'd felt energetic and capable of taking on new projects. I still spent entire days glued to the television, immobile except for caring for Stan, but I began to have good days too. I reached out to others more often, initiated conversations about difficult issues and felt my relationships begin to improve. I was no longer crabby with salespeople. I hung up the phone instead of yelling at phone solicitors.

Instead of the downward spiral that had consumed me, an upward spiral began. Little steps fed on themselves and led to bigger steps. I began to feel grateful.

Chapter 8

Marriage

Stan and I were lying in bed one morning and Stan asked, "Are you a woman?" "Yes," I answered. "Am I a man?" he asked. "Yes." "Are we married? "Yes." "Is there a piece of paper that says we're married?" "Yes." He reached for me and said, "I don't know your name, but I know I'm going to like you."

Experiencing a period of uncertainty in his career, Stan struggled with depression during his forties. He was living in California and it was the 1970s. Personal growth seminars were considered the solution to depression in that time and place. Stan embraced them enthusiastically and attended one almost every weekend for about a decade. When we met, many seminars and many years later, he could speak fluently of his fears and dreams. I contrasted his ability to my own reserve. Hiding, pretending and avoiding negative feelings had been a part of my family culture.

Driving together in the mountains one day, looking out at the canyons below and mountains in the distance, Stan was telling me about his fear...of me. His willingness to speak the truth startled me. Inspired by the beauty and vastness surrounding us, I promised myself to be completely honest and open with him, regardless of the outcome. Ignorantly, I'd stumbled onto the meaning of intimacy.

Our relationship grew, but neither of us was good with boundaries, both prone to give too much. Living on two coasts was a comfortable solution for both of us. Still not married, we maintained a honeymoon atmosphere for six years. Two telephone calls a day, morning and night, held the thread between visits. We spent about ten days together every month.

Eventually, dissatisfaction set in on my side. A hypnotic ideal of "marriage" took hold of me. "Take it to the next step," it's called. I began to feel that the bicoastal living symbolized our inability to come together as a team and to make a commitment to each other.

When I explained how I felt, Stan resisted. Throwing his clothes into my spare bedroom, I insisted that he sleep there or leave. He slept in the spare bedroom. Then suddenly a few weeks later he presented me with an engagement ring. A few weeks after that he told me he'd found a place for us to be married. Surprised, I discovered he'd arranged for a beautiful location overlooking the ocean.

Throughout most of history, money was an important consideration in marriage. It still is. I felt intelligent and worldly wise as Stan and I interrupted the wedding planning to prepare a simple prenuptial agreement. It kept our assets separate. His children would inherit his and his deceased wife's property and my children would inherit mine. The agreement didn't address long term disease. We assumed that any financial costs would be paid by the person with the disease. We didn't visualize one of us caring for the other for long periods of time.

After the diagnosis, I felt stupid. As much as I loved Stan, I felt I'd made a terrible mistake, wanting to marry him, insisting on it, then marrying him. I was in a position of caring for him without his caring for me. Marriages thrive on give and take. I take care of you and you take care of me.

Even through the dimness of the disease, Stan realized something was wrong. With his children's support, we worked out an arrangement where he helped me financially. My self-esteem improved.

"Enjoy your life together as long as you're having fun, then leave. Your finances are separate," advised an attorney I saw after my mother died. The advice seemed logical and made me feel strong and smart, but as the years went by I realized I could never leave. The attorney was describing what he would do, not what I would do. In the beginning I felt required to care for Stan. After my mother died and I realized what I would be facing, I could only commit to attempting to care for him. Now, looking back, I realize that in my heart, I'd always been fully committed.

I know a couple that has been married many years. They don't talk much. They never did. They don't do much together except go to family events. They enjoy being at home, quietly sharing the same space. They sit in front of the television every night holding hands and cuddling. They consider themselves happily married.

After the disease took hold, Stan's and my marriage wasn't very different from theirs. We had started by sharing our feelings. We'd enjoyed taking short trips together. Now we didn't do much of either. We shared the same space and watched TV. Sometimes we held hands and sat close. We took care of each other.

"You're pathetic," one of my daughters said when I told her I felt Stan and I had a good marriage. Stan was walking around the house opening bathroom doors when people were inside. She didn't see how marriage could be good with someone like that. She didn't see how I loved him.

A friend of mine is contemplating marriage. She's in her early sixties and has met a man the same age. They're in love. Stan and I visited her and we spent an afternoon together. When she talked about marriage I nodded toward Stan, whom I was feeding with a spoon. "This is marriage," I said. "You're looking at it." "Appealing" was the word she used. I was trying to discourage her, but she saw through my attempt. She saw how I really felt.

Chapter 9

Pushing Viagra

For several days Stan had followed me around the house repeating that he wanted to make love. I finally relented. We took off our clothes and went to bed. As I expected, nothing happened, and after a while I said, "It doesn't work the way it used to." "That's for sure," he agreed. I asked, "Remember when we used to make love all the time?" "With you?" he was shocked. "I just met you!"

"They didn't tell me there'd be a woman in my bed tonight!" my friend's husband said as he came out of the bathroom one evening and saw her already comfortable under the covers. They'd been married 40 years.

"Your name may be the same, but you're not my wife. Did you do away with her?" the same friend's husband repeated.

When asked how old he was, Stan always answered, "fortyish." Men with Alzheimer's often think their daughters are their wives and approach them sexually. A wife with Alzheimer's may accuse her husband of molestation when he touches her. If they have intercourse, she may be devastated by a perceived rape.

Sexuality is profoundly affected by Alzheimer's. Our sexuality is where we're most vulnerable, most easily hurt. With Alzheimer's the caregiver and family lose the comfort of roles. They become ordinary, just another face.

Stan's and my early intimacy was based on sharing feelings, a closeness that expressed in our sexual life. On learning Stan had Alzheimer's, I felt a distance grow between us. The proverbial elephant in the room materialized, forcing our relationship to shift and change profoundly around it. My sense of isolation grew.

Then he didn't recognize me.

The disconcerting ease with which Stan transitioned to thinking I was someone he'd just picked up disturbed me. Early in our relationship he confided in me his fantasy of having a harem. Now he had one, a new woman every day—me.

On the surface I playfully asked myself if he was being unfaithful. Was I being unfaithful? Emotionally, I felt an uneasy sense of violation.

As the disease progressed his ability to follow through sexually became more and more unreliable. He followed me around the house for most of the day wanting to make love and unable to understand why it didn't work when we tried.

"Some Viagra might improve our lifestyle," I told Stan's physician at the next visit. The physician blushed and looked uncomfortable but wrote a prescription. Once every week or so, I'd wake Stan early in the morning and give him his "vitamin" pill. After about an hour I'd wake him up again and "voila." He never connected the pill with our intimate moments together. He didn't know who I was, but I did find satisfaction knowing that I was meeting his needs. He was still my husband, lost somewhere between a man and a child. Besides, he stopped following me around the house all the time.

The diapers ended it. Walking toward me down the hall displaying his new "emergency underwear," I knew our sexual life was over.

"Take care of yourself," a physician told my friend. Dutifully she hired someone to stay with her husband while she walked on the beach, wiggled her toes in the sand and looked out over the ocean. "That's not what I meant," he said at the next visit. He was suggesting she find another relationship. People need to hear they're beautiful, handsome and valued. Many caregivers do find another relationship, sometimes sexual, sometimes not. I can't bring myself to consider it.

Occasionally we talk in the safety of strangers. Sitting on an airplane I shared the intimate details of my life with the woman sitting next to me. "Grief, ambiguity, losing your husband without closure," were the words she used to console me. It turned out she had a lot of experience. She was a psychotherapist specializing in caregivers.

Chapter 10

Razor Burn

I was taking a shower and heard a buzzing sound close by. Peeking out, I saw Stan brushing his teeth with his electric razor.

Stan seemed agitated and I asked him what the problem was. He said he was looking for his wallet. I helped him look for about fifteen minutes then asked him if he remembered what had happened to it. "Yes," he said, "I hid it."

Uncertainty, solving one problem after another, often the same problem in a different way, describe caring for someone with Alzheimer's. It's tragic and funny…Exhausting…Maybe rewarding. Finding someone to laugh with lightens the load.

Stan and I developed a new form of "intimacy" as the disease progressed. Parts of Stan's body that had once fascinated me, became familiar in a different way as I learned to deal with incontinence.

I'd brushed my daughters' long hair every day when they were young. When they complained that it hurt, I'd tell the story of the man who combed his hair once a year. It hurt so much he couldn't understand how anyone could do it every day. A cerebral type, with a background in computers and systems analysis, I was always moving toward the next task, hurrying through the tangles.

Stan had said he liked my "firm" touch. Inappropriate now, I had to learn to be more gentle, to slow down.

Stan shaved at least six times a day. I considered it his hobby though perhaps he wanted to be well groomed for the women in his harem. I wondered what the staff at the adult day care center thought as he appeared each day with a face full of cuts and decided he should try an electric razor. Electric razors consist of many little parts which fit together like a puzzle. Stan would take the razor apart after each shave and bring it to me to put back together. Frustrated, I moved to a safety razor and tried shaving him myself. The razor was not safe in my hands. Gazing at men's faces and pondering TV commercials for shaving products, I wondered at the mysterious world I'd entered. Finally calling my son in desperation, I learned the tricks to clear up the red bumps and cuts.

"Dental hygienists do this eight times a day. I can do it too," I told myself over and over as I struggled with floss and brushes. Stan had two cavities and refused to open his mouth for the dentist. To fill them would require general anesthesia. I cleaned his teeth every morning while he was still asleep in an effort to keep the cavities under control.

"Sucker List" is what I called the list or lists he was on. Never a wise investor, Stan enjoyed being courted by people who wanted his money. Early in the disease, before I moved to California and realized what was happening, his judgment failed and he gave away a significant part of his savings.

Arriving in California, I discovered the phone ringing at least three times a day, each time with a different slimy voice asking for Stan. He spent hours each day basking in the attention and refused to change his phone number of 45 years. Whenever the phone rang, I'd rush to sit next to him and listen. One day sitting next to him during a call, the man on the other end of the phone asked for his wife's social security number.

Stan turned to me and asked for it. I said, "I won't give it to you because it's a scam." Stan said, "My wife won't give it to you because it's a scam." The man hung up instantly. The glimmer of understanding lasted long enough for Stan to agree to change the phone number. I heard later that the woman who was assigned the old phone number by the telephone company screamed at anyone calling whom she didn't know.

Little tricks helped. I kept four identical wallets with fake IDs so when he hid one, I'd "find" another quickly. I pasted pictures of our home and family in a little book, his "memory book." For a time, he carried the book wherever he went and held it close. It calmed him down.

"We should be going north!" Stan shouted anxiously for 300 miles of a car trip. We were going north. "Exit here!" "Stop, stop!" "Pull over!" A few years later that phase passed and he enjoyed looking at the scenery.

I've read about Alzheimer's good days and bad days, but as a caregiver, I lived good moments and bad moments. What worked in one moment didn't work in the next. After attending a senior workout class, balancing and following along well, he'd be unsteady on his feet. If I let go of his hand, I'd worry that he'd fall and hurt himself.

Trying to maintain a normal life for him as long as possible, I took Stan with me to grocery stores and restaurants. Stan had always loved babies. When we went out, he sought them out enthusiastically, sometimes drooling as he rushed toward them. I was on constant alert for babies and small children wherever we went, often pulling him back just in time, apologizing profusely to the startled mother.

Early in the disease, as long as I could keep him away from babies, no one seemed to notice anything unusual. In fact, Stan was so good at small talk that people thought I was exaggerating the problem. After a few years, some people we saw in public places looked at him harder, noticed, understood and gave me a reassuring nod and supportive smile. When people no longer looked at me but stared at him, fixated, I knew I'd crossed an invisible cultural boundary. I wondered what to do. Should I protect others from their own discomfort or consider it my mission to help them face the reality of old age and death? Should I keep him home or take him out?

Caregivers of Alzheimer's patients become great actors and actresses, saying what is necessary to calm the patient down. They lie frequently saying things like, "Yes, the sky is green today." They pretend to understand gibberish and laugh at incomprehensible jokes. Or in desperation in the middle of the night, "Your mother wants you to go back to bed." "God said it's time to go to sleep." They also learn to live with truth.

Some people kindly offered to sit with Stan while I went out. Perhaps they visualized sitting next to him as he slept quietly or watched television. I doubt they visualized his jumping up suddenly, pulling down his pants and urinating in the dog's water bowl.

I was always surprised when people treated me like a normal person. They'd give me their e-mail address or phone number and say, "Let's keep in touch." They'd recommend a book they liked. I didn't feel normal at all. My life seemed to be unfolding in a different universe where things were not what they seemed, where disaster was just around the corner. I'd feel good for a while then have a crying jag that lasted a month.

As the years went by, I became more comfortable with caregiving. I like the word "seasoned." It can mean experienced or giving and improving flavor. The "flavor" of my life improved. I laughed more.

Chapter 11

Peeking Through

My daughter was caring for Stan and managing his incontinence. He didn't appear to know who she was and had been speaking incoherently most of the day. Suddenly, in a moment of clarity, he turned to her and said, "I'm sorry if I'm embarrassing you."

Stan was well progressed in the disease. Usually his words were incomprehensible. I paused to coo over my infant grandson as we were leaving my daughter's house. "Don't get any ideas!" he said clearly as though I might be interested in having a baby.

Alzheimer's is a strange disease. One moment Stan would appear comatose, vacant. The next moment he'd say something insightful. Uncertain what to expect at any moment, I struggled to make sense of my life, to find a higher meaning to help me cope.

Stan had never cared about higher meanings. Filled with a reverence for life and feeling a deep connection to nature, Stan's approach toward finding the meaning of life was simple, "You can't know anything for certain anyway, so why bother trying?" Not needing labels, he snickered when I used the "G" word, God. Yet his spiritual connection was deep. Once seeing a man on television comment that he prayed while jogging, Stan was surprised. "I don't even believe in God and I pray all the time!" he exclaimed.

Asking questions, "What's the meaning of life?" "Why are we here?" "What's really going on?" was my approach. So when Stan was diagnosed with Alzheimer's, he moved on contentedly as I struggled to make sense of it.

"It's for our generation to help people learn to live in the present," a friend of mine who works with Alzheimer's patients said. Stan's daughter who was searching for a natural cure focused on pollution and allergies.

I asked myself if I were playing a psychological game. Stan was living out his fantasy of a harem and experiencing safety and protection he never felt as a child. His growing inability to communicate reminded me of my emotionally distant father.

"How could a loving God let such a good person suffer so much?" one of my friends agonized. The last few years of his saintly mother's life had been heart wrenching. I didn't consider either Stan or me virtuous enough to be exempt from misery. I didn't feel singled out either, but I was angry.

Struggling with that anger in the beginning, I projected it onto an "Angry God." That didn't last long. The image of an angry, punishing God has never resonated with me. I love my children and would never knowingly inflict harm on them. A little "tough love" from time to time, but not eternal damnation. It made sense that God would feel the same way about me.

Several people suggested I view Stan as God and feel myself caring directly for God. I doubted that those people had ever cared for someone with Alzheimer's. Stan was not passive. He was frustrating. To associate Stan's behavior directly with God led me back to an "Angry God."

Trying to understand how others coped, I asked caregivers if the experience had changed them. They said they'd matured, grown up. Checkbooks, taxes and leaky roofs became easy. They also learned to live gracefully with ambiguity and to feel more compassion.

"I find it rewarding working with people with dementia," a professional caregiver told me. I noted that she went home every day to a normal family. Yet I was intrigued. There could be something I was missing.

Unable to find a meaning that satisfied me, I tried an approach that had helped me in the past. "Something good is going to come out of this," I'd repeat, assuming a plan or purpose to life. The worse the situation, the more difficult the problem, the more frequently and intensely I'd repeat it, changing the wording slightly to, "Something *really* good is going to come out of this."

This approach requires some positive energy, optimism, and acceptance. Confronted day after day with problems that felt insurmountable, I had little energy. Ten to fifteen years seemed too long to keep a positive attitude, to repeat my affirmation, but in better moments, I did.

I heard a story once about a preacher who visited nursing homes to minister to the patients. One woman was especially problematic. She had Alzheimer's and spent her days sitting in the corner of the sunroom crying uncontrollably. She worried about her sins and feared she was going to hell. The preacher tried to save her, explaining over and over, in every way he could think of, what she should do to be saved. Nothing worked. Then the preacher was diagnosed with Alzheimer's himself. Thinking back to that woman, he regretted how he'd handled the situation. He wished he'd held her hand or put his arm around her, comforting silently.

As time passed, I found that my frantic search for a meaning, the obsessive questions, died down. Instead of struggling to find the energy to repeat that something good would happen, I could feel positive changes in myself. From time to time Stan was peeking through the dimness of the disease. Parts of me I hadn't seen before were peeking through too. Like the preacher, I found myself developing more compassion for Stan, for relatives, for friends, and for myself. Like Stan, I felt more connection to life.

Chapter 12

The California Dream is Over

We were in a park and I was making a new friend.
"This is Stan, and I'm Joanne," I said. Stan stared at
me with astonishment and said "You are?"

After moving from southern California to the North-
east in February, Stan said, "Someone changed the
weather around here!"

Having a support system in place before you need it is
easier than trying to develop one when you do. New
friendships take time and energy as you work through
the awkward phase of not knowing what's safe to
share. I'd made new friends in California but still relied
more on old friends. The telephone proved invaluable.
A friend of over 20 years lost her husband suddenly
and was heartbroken. Struggling to get through each
day, she suggested that we call each other daily, a way
Stan and I had kept our connection when we lived 3,000
miles apart. I wondered if I could handle the commitment. I agreed anyway. It was a lifeline.

Stan's brother Sonny, almost 90, called often and
I developed a deep connection with him and his wife.

Sonny wept as Stan was less and less able to communicate. When Stan couldn't say much, Sonny talked to me, thanking me for what I was doing.

One of Stan's friends called occasionally. He had helped Stan through personal and professional difficulties and extended his concern to Stan's current situation. Always surprised by a call from someone I hardly knew, I appreciated hearing from him and my problems spilled out in answer to his questions. One day, as I was describing my loneliness living on the West Coast, he suggested that I move east.

"The California dream is over," he said. He was right. My reasons for moving west had passed. Stan no longer knew or cared where he was. His children had gotten their chance to be near him. California wasn't working for me.

Little by little my horizons were narrowing. Incontinence and swimming pools don't go well together. Going out was becoming more difficult. Stan was requiring a full time volunteer at the adult day care center to keep him from escaping. The staff was beginning to hint that I should look into other options.

There's a sort of "what's the point" attitude that takes over for friends and family on the periphery of caregiving. When the person with Alzheimer's stops recognizing them, is unable to talk on the phone, chat or go out to a restaurant when they visit, they stop calling and coming over. Our culture doesn't teach us how to relate to someone who doesn't respond.

I wanted to be closer to my children. I wanted to live in a community where I felt closely connected to others.

I'd visualized staying in California until Stan died, then returning to the East Coast. The years were going by. I reasoned that compromise is part of marriage. We had spent several years in Stan's world. Now it was my turn.

Experts on Alzheimer's strongly recommend against moving the patient after the disease has progressed beyond mild. It becomes impossible for them to learn anything new. The direction to the bathroom changes. The chair they sit on, table where they eat, suddenly disappear and they're left feeling confused, unable to adjust to the new arrangement. The disorientation can be permanent.

Sometimes terrified by the "small" people on the television whom he thought were six inches tall, Stan's disease had long before progressed into moderate and was moving toward severe. Still I decided to take the risk. Stan had known the house on the East Coast early in the disease. I hoped he'd remember it. Pulling myself together, and relying on help from others, I moved east.

Stan recognized the house and adjusted well. The guilt I felt about moving him lifted. Idealistically I'd always thought I should be happy wherever I lived, that happiness would bubble up from inside me if I had the right attitude. Maybe my attitude hadn't been right. Much of my sense of isolation melted away as I fit into a supportive community I knew well. Somehow through the upheaval of my time in California, my business had grown, and I settled into familiar responsibilities.

I saw my children often. My son and his wife saw my situation for themselves and were supportive and compassionate. I spent time with my granddaughter.

"You ruined my life," I'd said to Stan's youngest daughter when I'd first moved to California and problems had erupted in our relationship. Poor woman. I'd expected some sort of support from her that even I couldn't describe. It's not surprising that she'd been unable to give it. Then I'd overreacted and blamed her.

Later after my move east, she came to visit. Knowing she was critical of how I cared for her father, I wondered how to approach her visit. She disapproved of his diet, his medications and thought she could care for him better than I did. The situation speaks for itself, I realized. I'd let her do what she wanted, to care for him. When she arrived, I showed her a cot I'd set up for her in her father's bedroom. I showed her where the clean diapers were stored. She took him for a long drive that afternoon. When she returned from the drive, she'd changed her mind. She wanted to sleep in a different room. "I'm so sorry for the way I've treated you," she said. We hugged and I took over Stan's care again.

The reality of caring for an Alzheimer's patient is often not what people imagine. I'm grateful I never had to do body care for my father or my mother. I never had to try to sleep in the same room with them, calming them down if they became agitated in the night. I never had to lie to them.

Chapter 13

You'll Know When It's Time

I asked Stan if he loved me and he said, "I do now!"

Rarely can a family member care for an Alzheimer's patient at home until he dies. Not knowing when it might happen, but expecting to need one eventually, I visited a well-recommended care facility for Alzheimer's patients. As I was led on a tour by a smartly dressed sales woman, I heard howling. In the middle of an open area sat a man alone clutching his face and howling loudly. Staff walked by without looking at him and patients sat in wheel chairs transfixed by the television or dozing. "Oh, he just got out of the hospital," the woman remarked. "He's much better now."

I visualized Stan in that room, his heart breaking, trying to help the man and unable to, later becoming deadened to the howls.

In California, I'd wondered if the leader of a support group I'd attended got a commission from the in-home care service she worked for. She'd adamantly encouraged the caregivers in the support group to use her or another service rather than put the patient in a facility. Now I hoped she did and that it was huge. After visiting the care facility, I knew for certain I'd care for Stan at home as long as I possibly could.

"You'll know it when it's time and don't feel guilty," I'd heard in support groups. Some facilities are excellent. Everyone's circumstances are different. Some caregivers have full time jobs. Some are in poor health. Some are elderly. Reasons I've heard for putting a person in a facility are incontinence, escaping from the house and wandering, caregiver stress, and violent behavior. I knew one woman who couldn't stand that her husband watched Judge Judy all day, every day, on television. She put him in a facility to get some quiet. Caregiver and patient are two sides of a balance. Constant change requires constant adjustment. At some point no adjustment is enough keep the balance. That is when a caregiver realizes that a facility is the best option.

There have been moments when I thought I couldn't care for Stan anymore, but I've been able to move on.

"Lock up the knives. If there's a gun in the house, get rid of it," a neurologist had advised me. Alzheimer's patients sometimes think their caregivers are intruders. Sitting at my desk working, I'd felt Stan's hands suddenly wrap around my neck from behind. His grip was gentle but the position of his hands was threatening. Sneaking up from behind was threatening. Three times it had happened. "If you do that once more, I won't take care of you," I screamed after the third time. Some part of him heard, because it's been many years and he hasn't done it since.

Another time, he stopped eating and drinking. Questioning if the medications were having any effect at Stan's stage of the disease, a neurologist suggested weaning him off them as a test. Extreme agitation and a refusal to eat or drink was the result. Panicked, I started the medications again and called friends who were nurses. "I think he's dying. I can't handle this," I said. They suggested the obvious, blending his food and feeding him with a spoon. That crisis passed.

People speak in codes. "You can put him in a facility. There are some wonderful places," can be code for, "I'm not going to take care of him myself." "He's slipping away. He's gone." "The person I knew is no longer there," can be code for, "I can't connect with him. I feel helpless. I can't deal with this anymore." Most caregivers spend many hours with the patient. They know the essential person hasn't changed. They want to protect him as long as possible, care for him, and keep him at home. When the time comes to put him in a facility, even though they know it's time, it can be heartbreaking.

Stan had long before "graduated" from adult day care when Vincent appeared in our lives. I call him Saint Vincent. Vincent provides in-home care which gives me some respite. He helps me maneuver Stan up and down stairs. Vincent slaps Stan on the back good naturedly and makes him smile. In his 20s, I marvel at his comfort with the disease.

Stan is easy. When agitated, I tell him how wonderful he is. I feel it from my heart, and Stan sighs and relaxes. If he doesn't understand the words, I hold his hand or hug him.

Unlike many Alzheimer's patients, Stan "sundowns" only a few days a month. Patient's often become agitated after the sun goes down and can be awake all night. I try to prevent sundowning. In later years Stan showed a talent for dozing off during scientific meetings, awakening at critical moments to provide a valuable insight. During the day I let him practice this skill and let him nap only in a sitting position. He's tired enough in the evening that he sleeps well most nights.

Almost every day I ask myself if today will be the day that I'll know it's time for him to go to a facility. If I think it might be, I tell myself, "I'll wait until tomorrow to decide." So far the next day has been better, but I expect one day I'll know it's time.

Long ago Stan made his wishes clear. When he dies, we won't use heroic measures to keep him alive. It's unlikely that he'll say wise and inspiring things at the end the way my mother did. The wisdom and inspiration he's leaving behind are in my life and the lives of others.

Chapter 14

Changing

We live in the house where my grandparents and parents lived. On the wall of our bedroom is a picture I remember from my early childhood. It shows ocean and sky, turbulent. There's both a darkness and a light in the picture. Neatly encased in a frame, it still conveys a feeling of change, a storm is coming, or has just passed. It's dawn, or perhaps dusk.

I invited a friend over for tea one afternoon, an old fashioned custom. I served her anisette cookies and gingerbread men, and showed her the picture. "Unnecessary troubles," she said. "Creepy. Disturbing. How can you sleep with that in your bedroom?" I told her the picture felt like me, a neatly encased exterior with unsettling waves of emotion inside. I wondered if she'd continue to be my friend after I'd told her about the real me. She would, she said.

Have my troubles been unnecessary? Have I created more troubles than I needed to? I don't know. One thing I do know is that I repeated over and over that something good would come from my experiences, and it did.

I see little changes in myself. When Stan wanders around the house opening drawers and rummaging, determinedly carrying objects from one room to another, I don't panic, feel out-of-control. I'm pleased that he has an activity to keep himself busy and that he's getting some exercise.

I see big changes too. Most mornings I awaken looking forward to the day and wondering where it will take me. If I tire or become stressed in a few hours, I simplify immediately and use the strategies that keep me calm and focused.

Caregiving for Alzheimer's isn't something you "succeed" at in the sense of the word I once understood. Being there, just muddling through, is success. Turbulence and mood swings are part of the journey. Difficult decisions are heart wrenching. Nothing stays the same.

This story is not over. Stan is sleeping in the next room, snoring. He'll wake up soon and I'll shave him, floss and brush his teeth, and dress him. Stan may smile at me, his wonderful smile with crinkly eyes. He may not. If Vincent is here, he'll help. There will be good moments and difficult moments today. If today is like most days, I'll be happy.

Discussion Guide

Caring for Stan by Joanne Damours

Synopsis

Caring for Stan is the candid story of a woman suddenly confronted with her husband's Alzheimer's Disease. As problems erupt in managing the disease and in her relationships, she struggles to cope with loneliness and learn to be a caregiver. Touching on issues of family, marriage, addiction, sexuality, and religious beliefs, this book is thought provoking, funny at times, and an eye-opener into the world of Alzheimer's.

Discussion Questions

1. How do you feel about the author's use of humor in sharing her story? Do you think that humor is an appropriate way to address the difficult subject of Alzheimer's?

2. In what ways is caregiving for Alzheimer's similar to caregiving for a patient with cancer? Different?

3. How is the author's caregiving experience similar to that of other caregivers for Alzheimer's patients? Different?

4. Why is day-to-day care for Alzheimer's patients more difficult than for many other diseases? Describe some of the emotional conflicts a caregiver might experience.

5. Caregivers often focus on the patient, overlooking themselves. In what ways does the author succeed in taking care of herself? In what ways does she fail? How can caregivers care for themselves?

6. At what point or points in caregiving for Alzheimer's patients should the caregiver begin making decisions for the patient? What are the patient's rights? What are the caregiver's rights? What are the family's rights?

7. The author discusses sexual changes in relating to Alzheimer's patients. How do you think you'd handle those changes?

8. The author says caregivers lie frequently, yet learn to live with the truth. Do caregivers really lie? What does the author mean by learning to live with the truth?

9. Caregivers often experience a spiritual crisis while caregiving. Religious beliefs long held may or may

not help her cope. The author groped for meaning. Did she eventually find it? How can a person's religious beliefs help during difficult times? Hinder?

10. The author becomes conflicted about taking the patient out into public. How do cultural images of illness and death affect caregivers? How can caregivers respond? How can the public respond?

11. After her mother dies, the author is unsure if she can handle caregiving for her husband. What personality qualities helped her succeed? How did she have to change to succeed?

12. It's common for family members to have different opinions about how to care for an Alzheimer's patient. What problems did the author encounter in her family? How could she have handled the problems differently? How do other families react?

13. The author remembers her mother's very structured way of relating to her mother and mother-in-law. She comments that her children relate to her differently. Is that true for most families?

14. After the author's mother dies, she feels her children are trying to make decisions that are hers to

make. She asserts herself by saying, "I'm not dead yet." How can older people maintain their dignity as they age? How can children navigate their concerns about their parents to avoid confrontation?

15. The author states that people speak in codes and gives some examples. What are some other ways that people speak in codes about Alzheimer's? About death and dying? Why and when are codes useful? When are they not useful?

16. Many people say "You'll know when it's time" to put a patient in a facility. Does the time always come? How do you think you'd "know?"

17. The author feels she has a good marriage yet her husband has Alzheimer's. Why does she feel that her marriage is good? What makes a good marriage?

18. What does support mean? How did the author receive support? How could the author have received more support during her difficult times? What kinds of support can family members, friends, a community, anyone, offer a caregiver?

19. Did anything in the book surprise you? Has the book affected how you feel about caregiving? Caregivers? Yourself? Has it affected decisions you've made?

For Review

To order copies go to
www.caringforstan.com
or turn to the last page.

To order copies of this book or make comments go to
www.caringforstan.com

To order this book by mail
send $12.95 (USA) or $15.95 (Canada)
plus $5.75 for postage and handling to
Caleb Gardner Publications
P. O. Box 601
Nantucket, MA 02554-0601